Robert Louis Stevenson's Treasure Island

Written by Robert Louis Stevenson

Adapted by Benjamin Hulme-Cross

Illustrated by Vincent Shaw-Morton

Published by Pearson Education Limited, Edinburgh Gate, Harlow, Essex, CM20 2JE.

www.pearsonschools.co.uk

Text © Pearson Education Limited 2013

Designed by Vincent Shaw-Morton
Original illustrations © Pearson Education Limited 2013
Illustrated by Vincent Shaw-Morton

The right of Benjamin Hulme-Cross to be identified as author of this work has been
asserted by him in accordance with the Copyright, Designs and Patents Act 1988.

First published 2013

17 16 15 14 13
10 9 8 7 6 5 4 3 2 1

British Library Cataloguing in Publication Data
A catalogue record for this book is available from the British Library

ISBN 978 0 435 14410 4

Printed and bound in the UK by Ashford Colour Press

Acknowledgements
We would like to thank Bangor Central Integrated Primary School, Northern Ireland;
Bishop Henderson Church of England Primary School, Somerset; Bletchingdon Parochial
Church of England Primary School, Oxfordshire; Brookside Community Primary School,
Somerset; Bude Park Primary School, Hull; Carisbrooke Church of England Primary
School, Isle of Wight; Cheddington Combined School, Buckinghamshire; Dair House
Independent School, Buckinghamshire; Glebe Infant School, Gloucestershire; Henley
Green Primary School, Coventry; Lovelace Primary School, Surrey; Our Lady of Peace
Junior School, Slough; Tackley Church of England Primary School, Oxfordshire; and
Twyford Church of England School, Buckinghamshire for their invaluable help in the
development and trialling of the Bug Club resources.

Every effort has been made to contact copyright holders of material reproduced in this
book. Any omissions will be rectified in subsequent printings if notice is given to the
publishers.

Contents

CHAPTER ONE
Sea Dogs

I remember the captain's arrival as if it were yesterday. He was a tall, nut-brown man, with a greasy pigtail falling over his filthy blue coat. His face was scarred by what looked like an old sabre cut.

He stopped at the inn door and broke out into that old sea song I was to hear so many times:

"Fifteen men on the dead man's chest —
Yo-ho-ho, and a bottle of rum!"

Then he rapped on the door and, when my father appeared, called for a glass of rum. He looked around at the cliffs.

"You get much company, mate?" says he.

My father told him that no, sadly, there was very little company.

"Well, then," said he, "I'll stay here a bit. I can watch for ships and you can call me 'Captain'."

He threw four gold pieces on the floor.

"You can tell me when I owe more. Now, I'll take me old sea chest up to me room."

And that is how he came to be staying at the *Admiral Benbow*, my father's inn.

We learned very little about the captain. All day he sat on the cliffs with a telescope. All evening he sat in a corner near the fire and drank rum. We soon learned just to let him be.

But one day he took me aside.

"Boy," he whispers. "Want to earn a silverfourpenny every month?"

I said that sounded fine.

"Then keep your weather-eye open for a seafaring man with one leg. If that man appears, you let me know."

It dawned on me that our guest was in hiding.

The captain terrified our guests nightly. He would drink too much rum and sing his wild sea songs or tell frightening stories about walking the plank.

He stayed week after week until he owed my father a good deal of money. But if my father ever mentioned it the captain would roar and stare at my poor father until he left the room. My father had been seriously ill for a long while but I often think it was fear of the captain that drove him to his early grave.

Only one man ever stood up to the captain, and that was Dr Livesey.

The doctor had been checking on my father and he stayed a while afterwards to eat some dinner.

The captain, drunk and wild as always, prepared to roar out one of his songs.

He thumped the table, which we all knew meant we were to be silent. Dr Livesey looked up angrily.

"I have only one thing to say to you, sir," says the doctor. "Stop drinking so much rum, you dirty scoundrel!"

The furious captain sprang to his feet and drew out a knife.

The doctor spoke to him as before, over his shoulder.

"If you do not put away that knife, upon my honour, you shall be punished."

The captain soon resumed his seat, grumbling like a beaten dog.

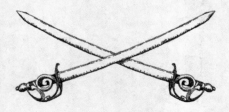

The trouble began early one frozen morning. The captain had walked to the beach. I was in the parlour when the door opened. The man at the door wore a cutlass, and he was missing two fingers.

"Come here, sonny," says he. "Is this here table for my mate Bill?"

I told him it was for the captain.

"Well," said he, "my mate Bill would be called the captain. He has a cut on one cheek. Now, is my mate Bill in this here house?"

I told him he was out walking.

"Then I had better wait for him," said the stranger. He hid behind the door, looking rather nervous.

At last, in strode the captain.

"Bill," said the stranger.

The captain spun round, looking pale. "Black Dog!" the captain gasped.

"Who else?" returned the stranger.

"Well," said the captain. "You've found me here, so what is it?"

"We'll sit down, if you please, and talk like old shipmates," said Black Dog. He told me to leave the room.

After some time I heard the captain's roar.

"No!" he cried. "If the law sinks me I'll

take you all down with me!"

There followed the clash of steel. The next instant I saw Black Dog in full flight, streaming blood from the left shoulder, chased out of the inn by the captain.

The captain walked back into the house.

"Jim," says he, "I need rum." But before I had a chance to move, the captain fell upon the floor. His eyes were closed and his face was a horrible colour.

By sheer good fortune, Dr Livesey arrived a moment later to visit my poor father.

"This man has had a stroke, as I warned him," said the doctor. The captain's shirt had torn at the sleeve, and on his great sinewy arm we saw two tattoos. One read 'Billy Bones', and the other showed a man hanging from a noose.

The captain opened his eyes. "Where's Black Dog?" he cried.

"Not here," said the doctor. "You have had a stroke, Mr Bones. I've told you once and I'll tell you again, stop drinking so much rum! Now, I'll help you to your bed."

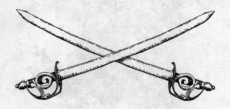

Around noon I took the captain a drink.

"Jim," he said, "will you bring me a glass of rum, matey?"

"The doctor —" I began.

"If I don't have a glass o' rum, Jim," he broke in, "I'll have terrible nightmares. They've begun already. I seen old Captain Flint in the corner there, behind you."

He was growing louder and this alarmed me, for my father was very low that day and needed quiet. But then the captain changed tack.

"Matey, did that doctor say how long I was to lie here?"

"A week at least," said I.

"Thunder!" he cried. "They'd have the black spot on me by then." He lay back for a while, silent.

"Jim," he said at length, "you saw Black Dog. He's bad, but not as bad as them that sent him. And if I can't get away from here they'll tip me the black spot. It's my papers they're after. If they come for me, you get over to that doctor. You tell him to bring every officer he knows to this inn and here he'll find the whole of Captain Flint's old crew from the *Walrus*. I was Flint's first mate, boy, and I knows where the treasure was buried. And I'm the only one as knows."

"But what is the black spot, Captain?" I asked.

"A summons, mate," said the captain grimly. And with that he fell fast asleep.

I began to worry about what to do, but soon all such thoughts left me. My father died that evening, and I could think of nothing else. The funeral was the very next day. I remember very little of it. My grief, I think, did something to my memory. But the day after the funeral I will never forget.

I was standing at the door in the afternoon, thinking about my father. I saw a blind man walking towards the inn, tapping in front of him with a stick. He was hunched and wore a sea-cloak with a hood over his head. He stopped by the inn.

"Will any kind friend tell me where I am?" he begged.

"You are at the *Admiral Benbow*," said I.

"I hear a voice," said he. "Will you give me your hand and lead me in?"

I held out my hand, and the hunched man gripped it like a vice. I tried to pull back, but the blind man hauled me closer to him with surprising strength. "Now, boy," he hissed, "take me to the captain."

I never heard a voice so cruel. I obeyed at once, walking straight in and across to our sick old pirate.

The captain raised his eyes. The expression on his face was a mix of fear and sickness.

"Now, Bill, sit where you are," said the blind man. "Hold out your left hand." Slowly, the captain obeyed.

The blind man placed something in the captain's hand and smiled horribly.

"Now, that's done," said the blind man, letting go of me. He turned and tapped his way to the door and out into the fog.

At length, the captain looked at the note in his hand.

"Ten o'clock!" he cried. "Six hours!", and he sprang to his feet.

But the next minute he put his hand to his throat, stood swaying for a moment, and then fell face to the floor. My mother ran downstairs. We made to help but it was in vain. Our old pirate was dead.

CHAPTER TWO
Blind Man's Bluff

The captain lay dead on the floor. We were owed some of his money, but the blind man was surely in wait nearby and his shipmates wanted everything the captain had. My mother and I stood in their way. We had to get out!

We dashed outside into the fading light and set off along the road. When we reached the nearest hamlet, it was dark. No help was to be found. We told the whole story, but at one mention of Flint's name all our neighbours recoiled. They knew more than I, for I had never heard of Flint before meeting the captain. My mother implored them, saying that without the money the captain owed us we were doomed. But the best they would do was send a party to fetch Dr Livesey and give us a loaded pistol to defend ourselves if we insisted on returning to the *Admiral Benbow*.

We raced back to the inn and bolted the door at once.

"He must have the key to his sea chest somewhere," said my mother, looking at the captain's corpse. I began to search. The first thing I found was a piece of paper, blackened on one side. The black spot! On the other side was a note. I read it out. "You have till ten tonight!"

"Perhaps the key's round his neck," suggested my mother, and she was right.

We hurried to his room, found the chest and threw open the lid.

Two things lay before our eyes: a bundle of papers tied up in oilcloth and a canvas bag that gave forth the jingle of gold.

Curse my mother's honesty! She insisted on taking only what was owed. This was a slow task, for the coins were from all over the world. We were only about halfway through the count when my heart froze. Outside on the lane I could hear the tap-tap-tap of the blind man's stick!

Then it struck sharp on the inn door, and we could hear the handle being turned and the bolt rattling. At last the tapping recommenced and, to our indescribable relief, faded away.

Still my mother insisted on making an honest count, and we argued over this until we heard, a short way off, a low whistle.

"I'll take the half I have," Mother said, jumping to her feet.

"And I'll take this to make us even," said I, grabbing the packet of papers.

We groped downstairs in the dark and fled the inn. Not a moment too soon! We could hear footsteps running towards the *Admiral Benbow*. We scuttled away towards the hamlet but had gone barely any distance when my mother stopped in the road, put a hand to her head and fainted on my shoulder.

We were just by a little bridge, still within earshot of the inn. Using the last of my strength I dragged my mother under the arch of the bridge, and there we hid.

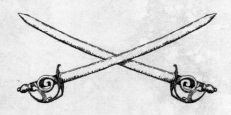

My curiosity was too much. I crawled back up the bank to watch events. Seven men stood outside the inn.

"In, in!" cried one, in a voice I recognised as the blind man's.

Four of them obeyed at once, two remaining on the road with the blind man. There was a pause, then a voice shouting from the house, "Bill's dead!"

"Search him, and get the chest!" the blind man ordered.

I could hear their feet rattling up our old stairs, then more shouting.

"Pew, they've been before us. Someone's turned the chest out."

"Is it there?" roared the blind man, Pew.

"The money's there."

The blind man cursed the money.

"Flint's map, I mean," he cried.

"We don't see it here nohow," returned the man.

"It's that boy. I wish I had put his eyes out!" cried Pew. "He was here no time ago – he had the door bolted when I tried it. Find him!" But before they moved, there came that low whistle again, twice repeated.

"There's Dirk again," said one. "Twice! We'll have to run, mates."

"Thunder!" cried Pew. "Dirk's a coward. That boy is close – find him, I say!"

"Hang it, Pew, we've got the money!" grumbled one.

Pew's temper overcame him, and he began lashing out with his stick at his companions. While the argument raged, a new sound reached my ears — it was the thunder of horses' hooves!

The pirates turned and scattered — all but Pew, who could not run. The horses swept down the slope at full gallop. Pew screamed and tried to run, but he stumbled and fell under the hooves of one of the horses, and that was the last of him.

I leaped to my feet and hailed the riders. They were law officers sent by one of the men from the hamlet, who rode behind. He took my mother off to the hamlet, and most of the men headed for the coast to try and apprehend the pirates. But by the time they reached the water's edge, a small boat was already a short way out to sea.

Back at the inn, though the pirates had taken nothing but the captain's money, they had destroyed the place in their search. The grim truth was that my mother and I were ruined. Even after the captain's contribution we did not have the money to mend the damage.

I could think of only one man to turn

to for help – Dr Livesey. One of the riders agreed to take me to him and we set off at a canter, me clutching at the oilskin packet in my breast pocket.

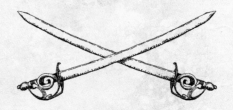

We rode hard all the way till we drew up before Dr Livesey's door. The house was all dark to the front and the maid informed us the doctor was at the squire's house.

I ran up the road to the old manor house and soon enough I was standing in front of Dr Livesey and Squire Trelawney.

"Good evening to you, Jim," said the doctor. "What brings you here?"

I spilled out my story and the two men sat astonished by the whole thing.

"So, Jim," said the doctor, "do you have what these miscreants were after?"

I gave him the oilskin packet. The doctor

put it quietly in his pocket.

"Squire," said Dr Livesey, "have you heard of this Captain Flint?"

"He was the bloodthirstiest buccaneer that ever sailed!" cried the squire.

"Well," said the doctor, "what I want to know is this: if what we have here is some clue to where Flint buried his treasure, will that treasure amount to much?"

The squire looked incredulous. "Open it, man!"

"Very well," said the doctor. He laid the packet on the table and opened it with a knife. It contained two things – a book and a sealed paper.

The book was full of accounts.

"This must have been Billy Bones's reckoning of his share of plunder!" said the squire. "But what is that paper?"

The doctor opened out a very detailed map of an island. Most intriguingly, there were three crosses marked on the map in red ink. Beside one cross were the words "Bulk of treasure here."

Over on the back of the map were various further directions. The squire and Dr Livesey were delighted.

"Livesey," said the squire, "tomorrow I start for Bristol. In three weeks' time we'll have the best ship and the best crew in England. Hawkins shall come as cabin-boy. You'll make an excellent cabin-boy, Jim. You, Livesey, are ship's doctor; I am admiral. We'll find this island and when we return we'll have money to roll in for the rest of our lives!"

"A warning, Trelawney," said the doctor. "We are not the only men who know of this paper. These fellows who attacked the inn tonight have sworn to get that money. Not one of us must breathe a single word of what we've found."

"Livesey," returned the squire, "you are right as always. I'll be as silent as the grave."

CHAPTER THREE
All Aboard!

A few weeks later we were in Bristol. The squire had paid for the *Admiral Benbow* to be restored and paid for a boy to work for my mother in my absence.

Then the squire had gone on ahead of Dr Livesey and me to Bristol, bought a schooner and hired a captain and a crew. This last he had done easily, he told us, for as soon as word got out that we were looking for treasure we had been the talk of the docks. That displeased Dr Livesey greatly, for he maintained this should have remained secret.

For my part, I was afraid of something else. The squire informed us that he had found a man who seemed to know every sailor in Bristol to help him hire the crew. This man was to serve as ship's cook on our voyage. The squire's description of the man gave me the shivers. His name was Long John Silver. He was, said the squire, a seafaring man with one leg.

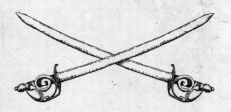

I was striding along Bristol docks with a note the squire had given me, addressed to John Silver. In my most fearful moments I imagined this Silver was the man the captain had been so afraid of. But even if he were that man, he would not know who I was.

I looked about the docks as I walked, thrilled by the sight of so many ships, and rough-looking men of the sea, and full of dreams about our voyage. I carried on this way until I came to John Silver's tavern, the *Spy-Glass*.

It was a bright, clean place. The customers were loud seafaring men, and I hung at the door, almost afraid to enter.

As I was waiting, a man came out of a side room, and at a glance I was sure he must be Long John Silver. His left leg was cut off close by the hip, and he carried a crutch, which he managed with wonderful skill, hopping about upon it like a bird. He was very tall and strong, with an intelligent face. He seemed in the most cheerful spirits, whistling as he moved about among his customers.

My fears vanished. I had seen the captain and Black Dog and the blind man, Pew, and I thought I knew what a pirate was like – very different to this pleasant landlord. I walked straight up to him.

"Mr Silver, sir?" I asked, holding out the squire's note.

"Yes, my lad," said he, "and who may you be?"

Then, as he saw the squire's letter, he gave a start.

"Oh!" said he, offering his hand. "I see. You are our new cabin-boy."

He took my hand in his large firm grasp.

Just then one of the customers rose suddenly from his table and made for the door. I recognised him at a glance. He was missing two fingers.

"Oh," I cried, "stop him! It's Black Dog!"

"Harry, run and catch him!" cried Silver.

One of the customers by the door ran off in pursuit.

"Who did you say he was?" asked Silver. "Black what?"

"Dog, sir," said I. "Has Mr Trelawney not told you of the pirates? He was one of them."

"A pirate! In my house!" cried Silver. "See here, now, Hawkins, this ain't going to look too pretty when we tell the squire – a pirate in my house and we let him get away!" He patted me on the back and I felt quite flattered as he went on. "You're just a lad, but you're as smart as paint. I seen that when you first come in."

Then, all of a sudden, he stopped, and his jaw dropped as though he had remembered something.

"The dog!" he burst out. "Three goes o' rum! Why, shiver my timbers, I let him get away without paying!" And, falling on a bench, he laughed until the tears ran down his cheeks. I could not help joining in, and we laughed together, peal after peal, until the tavern rang.

"Why, what a precious old sea-calf I am!" he said at last, wiping his cheeks. "You and me should get on well, Hawkins, but come on now, we should go and report all this to Mr Trelawney."

Long John was a fine companion as we walked, telling me about the different ships that we passed, or repeating a nautical phrase till I had learned it perfectly. I began to see that here was one of the best of possible shipmates.

When we had found Dr Livesey and Mr Trelawney, Long John told the story from first to last. The two gentlemen regretted that Black Dog had got away, but we all agreed there was nothing to be done, and after he had been complimented, Long John took up his crutch and departed.

"All aboard by four this afternoon," shouted the squire after him.

"Aye, aye, sir," cried the cook.

"Well, squire," said Dr Livesey, "I like this John Silver very well."

"We couldn't find a better man to sail with if we scoured the whole of England," declared the squire.

"Now, the time has come," said the doctor. "Take your hat, Jim, and we'll see the ship, the *Hispaniola*."

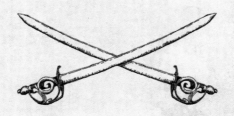

After a short time on deck we headed below into the cabin and had barely sat down when there was a knock at the door and we were joined by the ship's captain. The squire's face darkened.

"Well, Captain Smollett, what have you to say? All well, I hope?"

"Well, sir," said the captain, "better speak plain. I don't like this cruise and I don't like the crew you hired."

"Possibly, sir, you don't like me either?" says the squire.

Here Dr Livesey cut in.

"Why don't you like this cruise, Captain?"

"First, I don't know where we are headed and I await your instructions," said the captain. "But now I find that the crew knows more than I do."

"Next," said the captain, "I learn from the crew we are going after treasure, in secret. It's my belief that this will turn into a close run between life and death."

"True," replied Dr Livesey. "It's a risk. Next, you say you don't like the crew."

"I should have had a hand in choosing them," said the captain.

"Any offence was unintentional," replied the doctor. "You had better tell us what you want."

"I have three points to make," said Captain Smollett. "First point: store the powder and guns close to where we will sleep and away from the crew. Second point: you are bringing four of your own men with you, Mr Trelawney. These men you have known for years. Why not have them sleep near us and not with the rest of the crew?"

"Anything else?" asked Mr Trelawney.

"Yes," said the captain. "There's been too much blabbing already."

"Far too much," agreed the doctor.

"I'll tell you what I've heard myself," continued Captain Smollett. "You have a map of an island. There's crosses on the map to show where treasure is. And I know the exact location of the island."

"I never told that to a soul!" cried the squire.

"The crew know it, sir," returned the captain. "Anyhow, I don't know who has this map, and I don't want to know."

"Sir," said the doctor. "You wish us to keep the map hidden, to store the guns where we control them and to man this part of the ship with our own men. In other words, you fear a mutiny."

"I didn't say that," said Captain Smollett. "I just ask you to take precautions."

"I've heard enough!" shouted the squire. "I will do as you desire, but I think the worse of you, captain."

"You'll find I do my duty," said the captain, and with that he took his leave.

"Trelawney," said the doctor, "I believe you have managed to get two honest men on board with you – Smollett and John Silver."

"Silver, if you like," cried the squire, "but as for that intolerable captain, his conduct is unmanly and cowardly!"

"Well," says the doctor, "we shall see."

CHAPTER FOUR
The Voyage

A little before dawn next morning, the boatswain sounded his pipe and the crew began to man their stations.

"Now, mates," said Long John. "A song!" He broke out in the words I knew so well:

"Fifteen men on the dead man's chest —"
And then the whole crew took up the chorus:
"Yo-ho-ho, and a bottle of rum!"

The sails began to fill and, before I could lie down to snatch another hour of slumber, the *Hispaniola* had begun her voyage.

It soon became clear that all the crew respected and even obeyed Long John Silver, and he was always kind to me.

"Hawkins," he would say, "come and have a yarn with John. Nobody more welcome than yourself, my son. Here's my parrot – Cap'n Flint I calls him, after the famous pirate." And the parrot would screech, "Pieces of eight! Pieces of eight!"

In general, everyone was content. The crew were treated well, and there was always a barrel of apples standing open for anyone to help himself. Had it not been for that barrel we might all have perished horribly.

This was how it came about.

We were nearing the end of the long voyage, expecting to sight the island soon.

Just after sundown, I had finished my work and fancied an apple. I ran up on deck and made for the barrel. Finding it almost empty, I climbed inside, sat down and began to eat.

A few minutes later I heard Silver's voice nearby, very quiet. Before I had heard a dozen words I was trembling with fear.

"We was a fine crew," said Silver. "Flint was captain. Billy Bones was first mate. I was quartermaster before I lost my leg to a broadside. The same battle cost old Pew his eyes. But I saved two thousand pound while under Flint."

"Ah!" cried another – it was the youngest of the crew, full of admiration for Silver. "He was the flower of the flock, was Flint!"

"You look here," said Silver. "You're young, you are, but you're as smart as paint. I seen that when I set my eyes on you, and I'll talk to you like a man."

You can imagine how I felt. Long John Silver was one of Flint's men of old, and a dangerous pirate, and he was flattering this young seaman in the same words he had used with me.

"Here it is about us pirates," Silver went on. "We lives rough, and we risk hanging, but when a cruise is done it's hundreds of pounds in your pockets. Now, I'm fifty, and I been putting all the gold away for years. When I get back from this cruise, I've enough to set up as a gentleman. And how did I begin? Crewing before the mast, like you!"

"Well, John," replied the lad, "I'm with you, and here's my hand on it."

I began to understand what was happening. Silver was persuading the seaman to join him as a pirate.

A third man strolled up and sat down near Silver.

"Here's what I want to know, John," said the newcomer. I recognised the voice of our coxswain, Israel Hands.

"When do we take them on? Smollett's bossed me long enough, by thunder!"

"By the powers!" cried Silver. "The latest we can, that's when. Captain Smollett sails the ship for us. The squire and doctor have the map. They find the treasure for us. Then we'll strike. Thunder! You men have no brains!"

"But," asked the youngest of the three, "when we do strike, what are we going to do with 'em?"

"Duty is duty, mates," replied Silver. "We kill 'em all! Now you, lad, fetch me an apple out of that barrel."

You may fancy the terror I was in! But then Israel Hands said, "Stow that! Let's have a go of the rum."

The young lad ran off to fetch some rum, and I heard Hands whisper to Silver, "Not all of them will join us, John."

Not another word was uttered, for just then the lookout shouted, "Land ho!"

There was a great rush of feet across the deck and I jumped out of my barrel in time to join Dr Livesey in the rush.

The island lay before us in the moonlight, three sharp hills thrusting up out of the ocean.

"Has any one of you ever seen that island?" asked Captain Smollett.

"I have, sir," said Silver. "I've stopped there with a trader many years ago."

"Good man," said the captain. "I may ask you for some help steering us in later."

Silver looked over and winked at me before hopping over. I tried hard not to shudder.

"Ah," says he, "this island's a sweet spot for a lad to get ashore on. When you want to go exploring, you just ask old John, and he'll cook up a snack for you to take along."

Clapping me in the friendliest way upon the shoulder, he hobbled off and went below.

Captain Smollett, the squire and Dr Livesey were talking together. Dr Livesey called me to his side. He had left his pipe below decks and wanted me to fetch it.

"Doctor, let me speak," I said. "Get the captain and squire down to the cabin, and find an excuse to send for me. I have some terrible news."

His eyes widened. "Thank you, Jim," said he, loudly, "that was all I wanted to know."

With that, he turned on his heel and rejoined the other two. They spoke together for a little, then went below, and, soon after, sent word that I was wanted in the cabin.

I found them seated round the table, a bottle of Spanish wine and some raisins before them.

"Now, Hawkins," said the squire, "you have something to say. Speak up."

I told them the details of Silver's conversation.

"Jim," said Dr Livesey, "take a seat."

They poured me out a drink and all three told me that they believed they owed me their lives.

"Now, captain," said the squire, "you were right about this crew, and I was wrong. I await your orders."

Captain Smollett nodded. "First point," he began, "we can't turn back; they would strike at once. Second point, we have some time until this treasure's found. Third point, Silver has not corrupted the whole crew and there will be two sides to this battle.

Now, sir, I propose we find those that are loyal, and bide our time, and then attack the pirates. If we wait for them to attack we are done for!"

"Upon my honour, Captain," declared the squire sincerely, "I should never have doubted your value."

"How many are on our side?" asked Dr Livesey.

"Three of the squire's own men," reckoned the captain, "and the four of us make seven, counting Hawkins here. But what of the honest crew?"

"Impossible to say," said the squire.

"Jim, here," said the doctor, "can help us find those of the crew who we can rely on. The men are not shy with him, and Jim has keen eyes and ears."

"Hawkins, I put all my faith in you," added the squire.

I was beginning to feel desperate. Seven of us stood between a vast stash of treasure and a crew of the most ruthless pirates who had ever sailed.

Worse still, the captain, the doctor and the squire were now relying on me to improve our odds!

CHAPTER FIVE
The Man of the Island

When I came on deck next morning, the island' looked very different. In the silver moonlight it had appeared enticing and mysterious. Now it seemed hard and forbidding. Grey trees, dark rock and hard pounding surf gave an air of menace. There was no sign that any man had ever walked this land, though I knew from the map that there was somewhere a house and stockade.

Silver directed the *Hispaniola* through a very tight channel into a wide natural harbour that was almost land-locked. The crew were beginning to drop all pretence of loyalty, and orders were received with dark looks and grumbles. The threat of mutiny hung in the air. I feared that my task of finding the loyal men was to prove fruitless.

We held a council in the cabin.

"The men are tense. If I give one more order," said the captain, "the battle will begin at once. And if I don't give any orders then Silver will see that we have sensed the danger."

"There is only one thing to be done," he went on. "We know Silver wants to wait until the treasure is found before he strikes. I will tell the men they can go ashore for the day. By the time they return Silver will have pacified them."

It was decided. The captain went on deck and addressed the crew.

"Lads," said he, "an afternoon ashore will hurt nobody. I'll fire a gun half an hour before sundown."

Six of the crew decided to stay on board, and the remaining thirteen, including Silver, began to embark in the shore boats.

To this day I do not know what came over me at that moment, but I decided to go ashore with the crew. I slipped over the side and into one of the boats. Silver was in the other boat, but he saw me and immediately I regretted my rash impulse. I was leaving all my friends on the ship!

By the time the boat reached the shore I was convinced that the pirates would cut my throat when we were out of sight of the ship. Sweating, I leapt out of the boat and sprinted into the trees.

I could hear Silver in the other boat shouting after me, but as you may imagine I ran until I could hear him no longer.

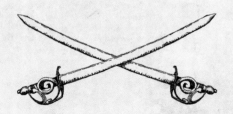

Though I was constantly aware of the danger I was in, I could not help but also be excited. I had slowed to a walk and was moving through thick trees, and then across wide sand dunes, surrounded by strange, exotic birds and plants. Ahead of me, the biggest of the three hills of the island looked more like a mountain now and for a short while I felt that I was exploring, without a care in the world.

But then, not far off to my left, I heard men's voices.

I crouched down under a bush and waited, but the voices did not draw any closer or further away. Presently I decided to approach and see what I could learn of the pirates' plans.

I crept slowly to the edge of the thick trees and peered out. This was at the shoreline but some way from where I had jumped out of the boat. I could see Silver and one other man sitting on the sand.

"I won't do it John!" said the man. "Not me, I won't!"

Then, a way behind me, I heard a man cry out in pain and give a long, drawn-out scream that stopped suddenly. My blood fairly froze in my veins!

The man who was talking to Silver jumped up in alarm.

"What's this?" he cried.

"That will be Alan," said Silver, still sitting. "Now lad, are you sure you won't be joining with us?"

"Curse the lot of you!" said the man defiantly, and he turned to walk away.

Quick as lightning, Silver leapt to his feet and hurled his crutch at the man like a spear. The man fell forward into the sand and I shrank back to hide deeper in the trees. I heard awful sounds, and when I looked again the man was lying in a pool of blood, and Silver was standing over him, a knife in his hand.

The sounds of the island grew louder and then fainter. The sand and the trees whirled about my head and I fainted. Not for long! A moment later I came around to hear John

Silver giving a long blast on his whistle.

So, I thought, *they have killed two of the honest men, and next they will come for me!*

I crawled back towards more open ground, while Silver and the others called to each other through the trees. As soon as I felt I was far enough away I stood and ran blindly, wild with terror. I do not know how long I ran, but presently I noticed that the air had changed a little, and the trees looked taller and healthier.

As I began to take in my new surroundings, a fresh danger brought me to a standstill with a thumping heart.

Up ahead I saw a dark, shaggy figure leap behind a tree. I thought of wild beasts and cannibals, and for a moment wondered whether Silver and the pirates were a preferable danger. But then I remembered my pistol, and taking a deep breath I walked towards the tree.

The figure reappeared. I could see now that it was a man, but not like any I had ever seen. He was stooped, and wild, and his hair hung down almost to his waist. He hesitated, then ran towards me and fell on his knees, looking up at me imploringly.

"Who are you?" I asked.

"Ben Gunn," he answered, and his voice sounded like a rusty lock. "I'm poor Ben Gunn I am, and I haven't spoke these three long years."

"Three years!" I cried. "Were you shipwrecked?"

"Nay, mate," said he. "Marooned. They left me here three years ago. I've lived on goats and berries since then. You mightn't happen to have a piece of cheese about you, now? No?"

"If ever I can get aboard again," said I, "you shall have cheese by the stone."

"If ever you can get aboard again, says you?" he repeated. "Why, now, who's to stop you?"

"Not you," was my reply.

"And right you are," he cried. "Now what do you call yourself, mate?"

"Jim," I told him.

"Jim," he said, looking furtively around him. "I'm rich."

And then his face darkened.

"Now, Jim, you tell me true — that ain't Flint's ship down there?" he asked.

I began to believe that I had found an ally, and I answered him at once.

"It's not Flint's ship, and Flint is dead, but there are some of Flint's crew aboard — worse luck for the rest of us."

"Not a man with one leg?" he gasped.

I told him the whole story of our situation. He heard me with the keenest interest, and when I had done he patted me on the head.

"You're a good lad, Jim," he said, "and you're in trouble, ain't you? Well, you just put your trust in Ben Gunn. Now, would you think your squire might spare me some of the treasure if I were to help him find it?"

I told him he would.

"Well, here's my story," said he. "I was on Flint's ship when he buried his treasure on the island, though none of us knew where. Some years later I was on another ship and we passed the island. I told the crew we could find Flint's treasure so we came ashore to look for it. We searched and searched and didn't find it, and they grew angry. Then they gave me a spade and a gun and told me I could stay and look, and they sailed away and left me here, the dogs." He broke off. "What's that?" For just then, the island awoke and bellowed to the thunder of a cannon.

"They have begun to fight!" I cried. "Follow me."

We began to run towards the anchorage.

The cannon-shot was followed after a considerable interval by a volley of gunfire.

We ran on, and some time later I saw the strangest sight. Ahead of us, above some trees, the Union Jack fluttered in the breeze.

CHAPTER SIX
The Stockade

As soon as Ben Gunn saw the flag he came to a halt, stopped me by the arm and sat down.

"Now," said he, "there's your friends. The pirates would have flown the Jolly Roger."

"True enough," I answered, though I could not understand how they had got there.

"Jim," he continued. "I'll be leaving you. Perhaps you'll tell your captain that Ben Gunn has a proposition for him to his advantage and mine. Perhaps you'll tell him to send someone to talk to me. I'll not walk into a camp until I knows I can trust everyone there. Anyhow, if he wants to speak, he can find me tomorrow afternoon, same place I found you."

And with that, he turned and sprang back the way we had come.

About half an hour later I walked out of the trees and approached the flag. It flew atop a log house, surrounded by the stockade. This tall fence created a large protected area outside the house.

Inside I was warmly welcomed by Dr Livesey and the others. There were six of them: the doctor, the squire, the captain and three loyal men from the ship: Hunter, Joyce and Gray. The doctor told me that they had come ashore with some food, guns and powder, looking for the stockade which they knew from the map should be here. They thought it would be an easier position to defend than the ship. He said they had left five pirates on board the *Hispaniola*, without guns or a boat to get to shore. But they had forgotten about the cannon, and the pirates onboard ship were firing at the flag, though were not hitting the house. No doubt Silver and the others would be joining them on board before long!

I had soon told my story and began to look about me.

There was a huge pile of guns and cutlasses on the floor. The log house had a few loop holes in its walls, through which to fire upon unwanted visitors.

I began to feel much better. The doctor was right – with a defence like this we might have a chance!

Captain Smollett kept us busy through to nightfall, clearing and keeping watch and cooking. We heard no more from the pirates that day, but as I lay down to sleep that night I could hear them down on the beach, roaring out their songs.

I woke next morning to a bustle and the sound of voices.

"Flag of truce!" I heard someone say, and then with surprise, "It's Silver himself!"

I ran to a loophole in the wall.

Sure enough, there he was outside the stockade, waving a white flag.

"Cap'n Silver, sir, wishing to come on board and make terms," he shouted.

"Captain Silver! Don't know him. Who's he?" cried the captain.

Long John answered. "These poor lads have chosen me cap'n, after your desertion, sir. May we speak safely?"

"My man," said Captain Smollett, "I have not the slightest desire to talk to you. If you wish to talk to me, you can come. I won't harm you."

Silver advanced to the stockade, swiftly threw over his crutch and scrambled over to our side.

"If you have anything to say, my man, better say it," said the captain.

"Well, here it is," said Silver. "We want that treasure, and we'll have it — that's our point! You would just as soon save your lives, I reckon, and that's yours. You have a chart, haven't you?"

"That's as may be," replied the captain.

"Now," resumed Silver, "here it is. You give us the chart to get the treasure by, and we'll offer you a choice. Either you come aboard ship along with us, once the treasure is stowed, and then I'll give you my word to drop you somewhere safe ashore. Or if that ain't to your fancy, then you can stay here, you can. We'll divide food with you, man for man, and I'll send the first ship I sight here to pick you up."

Captain Smollett rose from his seat. "Is that all?" he asked.

"Every last word, by thunder!" answered John. "Refuse that, and you've seen the last of me but musket-balls."

"Very good," said the captain. "Now

you'll hear me. If you'll come up one by one, unarmed, I'll promise to take you home to a fair trial in England. If you won't, I'll see you all to Davy Jones. You can't find the treasure without us. You can't sail the ship without me — I'm your navigator. You can't defeat us in this stockade — this place is a fortress. And in the name of heaven, I'll put a bullet in your back when next I meet you. Now get back to your dogs!"

Silver's face was a picture; his eyes started in his head with wrath.

"Them that die'll be the lucky ones," he shouted. And with that he stumbled off, climbed over the stockade and disappeared among the trees.

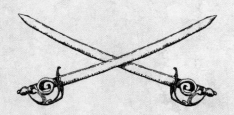

As soon as Silver disappeared, the captain turned to us and spoke.

"My lads," said he, "I've given Silver a broadside. I pitched it in red-hot on purpose, and before the hour's out, as he said, we shall be attacked." He strode around the house, planning the defence.

"Doctor, you will guard the door," he resumed. "See, and don't expose yourself; keep within, and fire through the porch. Hunter, take the east side, there. Joyce, you stand by the west, my man. Mr Trelawney, you and Gray will take the north side. Now listen: if any of them can get up close to the house they'll fire on us through the loopholes and we'll die like rats in a barrel.

"Hawkins, neither you nor I are much account at the shooting. We'll stand by to load and bear a hand."

Just as the full force of the sun came down for the first time that morning, the pirates struck.

Suddenly, with a loud cry, a little cloud of pirates leaped from the woods on the north side and ran straight on the stockade. At the same moment, a huge volley of shots rang out from the woods all around. Clearly the pirates were well armed now. We learned later that Silver had smuggled a small arsenal aboard the *Hispaniola* and ashore in the boats.

The pirates swarmed over the fence like monkeys. The squire and Gray fired again and again; three men fell, one forwards into the enclosure, two back on the outside. But of these, one was evidently more frightened than hurt, for he was on his feet again in a crack and instantly disappeared among the trees.

The other four were now inside our defences and running towards the house.

One grabbed Hunter's musket and punched him out cold. At the same moment another fell on Dr Livesey at the door with a cutlass.

"Out, lads, out, and fight 'em in the open! Cutlasses!" cried the captain.

I snatched a cutlass from the pile and raced outside. I came face to face with one of our attackers, his arm raised over his head to strike me with a cutlass. I slipped and rolled down the hill towards the stockade, and then the doctor was shouting, "We have them, lads! Back to the house."

Gray had killed the man who was attacking me. Another had been shot through one of the loopholes. A third Livesey had slain, and the fourth was making good his escape.

Back at the house we saw the price we had paid for victory. Hunter lay beside his loophole, stunned; Joyce lay dead on the floor. Right in the centre of the house, the squire was supporting the captain, one as pale as the other.

"The captain's wounded," said Mr Trelawney.

"Have they run?" asked Mr Smollett.

"All that could, you may be bound," returned the doctor, "but there's five of them will never run again."

CHAPTER SEVEN
The Coracle

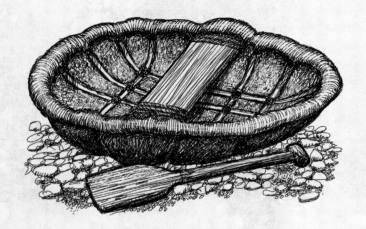

We saw no more of the pirates that day. The captain had been shot through the calf and through the shoulder, and the doctor tended to his wounds. Hunter, I am sorry to say, never regained consciousness.

A little after noon, the doctor announced he was walking to meet Ben Gunn, and he set off through the trees alone. This left the rest of us surrounded by bodies in the sweltering heat. For the second time, a truly mad notion came into my head. Ben Gunn had spoken of his little boat, and it seemed to me a fine idea to find the boat and then, if it could be done without detection, slip over to the *Hispaniola* that night and cut her adrift. I hoped that the ship would wash up ashore somewhere awkward. For now, we had the map and the pirates had the ship. Anything that weakened their position would strengthen ours.

Looking about me, I filled my pockets with rations and took a brace of pistols. That done, I waited for a moment when the others were distracted and slipped over the stockade into the shelter of the trees.

The previous day, as we ran towards the Union Jack, Ben Gunn had shown me the white rock near which his boat was hidden. Now I made my way back towards it as quietly as I could, for I did not know where Silver might have stationed his sentries.

I came to the place after an hour or so. The boat was the most primitive craft I have seen in my life: a tiny wooden frame covered in stretched goat skins, with a small paddle laid against the side. I have learned since that this sort of craft is called a coracle. It looked the feeblest of boats, but I thought it should hold a small lad on the calm, sheltered water of the harbour in which the *Hispaniola* lay.

I carried the boat – for its main advantage was that it was very light – to the edge of the trees and set it down to wait for nightfall. Out in the harbour I could see the *Hispaniola*, the Jolly Roger flying from her mast.

When the darkness was complete, I picked up the little boat and stumbled down to set it in the water. I climbed in and pointed towards the dim shadow of the *Hispaniola*, only now beginning to wonder whether I was heading to my death.

The coracle proved seaworthy and safe, but very difficult to steer, and I found I could do little but turn in circles. By good fortune though, the tide bore me out straight towards the ship, and in no time at all I was up alongside her and pulling quietly towards the anchor rope, which I proceeded to slice, strand by strand, with my pocket knife.

Almost at once the ship began to slip away with the tide, and as it passed me a trailing rope brushed over my hand. I grabbed hold, thinking I would take a look inside the cabin through the stern window, and pulled myself in. I had begun to wonder whether anyone was aboard, because none had shouted the alarm, but one look explained all. As I stood in my coracle and peered into the ship's cabin, I saw that the two watchmen, Israel Hands and another, were locked together in a deadly brawl, hurling oaths and plainly drunk.

I let go immediately, thinking I would leave them to their fate. Only then did my predicament become clear. The tide was now carrying the *Hispaniola*, not to shore, but out through the narrow channel towards the open sea. And my coracle, tiny though she be, was being carried that way also.

I tried to row towards land but every move tipped the coracle so violently that I feared I would drown. Eventually I lay down flat in the bottom of that wretched craft and began to pray. I must have lain like that for hours, until exhaustion defeated fear and sleep came upon me.

It was broad day when I awoke to the sound of sails thumping and slapping. I peered over the edge of the coracle and my heart sank. Some way from the island, I was lurching atop huge waves out on the open sea. I turned and looked in the other direction, and what I saw made me leap to my feet.

Barely a stone's throw away was the *Hispaniola*. Some of the sails had been hoisted but were flapping to and fro in the wind. This was the sound that had woken me. As I stood up, the coracle tipped alarmingly and slid down the side of a huge wave, straight towards the ship.

A moment later and I would hit the *Hispaniola*. My craft would sink and I would be drowned. Next, the bowsprit, pointing out from the front of the ship, was over my head. I sprang up again. With both hands I caught hold of the bowsprit.

As I clung there panting, a dull blow told me that the ship had charged down upon and struck the coracle and that I was now left without retreat on the *Hispaniola*.

CHAPTER EIGHT
Israel Hands

I fell head foremost on the deck and prayed that Hands and his companion had not heard me. Crawling stealthily along the deck away from the bow I soon saw that the danger was not so great.

There were the two watchmen, sure enough. One lay dead on his back, eyes wide, with his arms stretched out and his teeth showing through his open lips. Israel Hands was propped against the bulwarks, his chin on his chest, his hands lying open before him on the deck, his face white.

I could not be certain that Hands was dead. While I was looking and wondering, he turned partly around and gave a low moan.

"Come aboard, Mr Hands," I said ironically.

He rolled his eyes round heavily, but he was too far gone to express surprise. All he could do was to utter one word: "Brandy."

I found him some. He must have drunk a pint before he took the bottle from his mouth.

"Aye," said he, "by thunder, but I wanted some o' that!"

"Much hurt?" I asked him.

He merely grunted.

"Well," said I, "I've come aboard to take possession of this ship, Mr Hands, and you'll please regard me as your captain until further notice. Now, first we will be rid of that flag." So saying I hauled down the Jolly Roger and cast it into the sea.

Hands watched me keenly and slyly, his chin all the while on his breast.

"I reckon," he said at last, "I reckon, Cap'n Hawkins, you'll want to get ashore now. And

I don't reckon you'll sail this ship without my instruction. S'pose we talks."

We made our bargain immediately. I told Hands we were not headed for the harbour we had come from, but would sail in at the north end of the island, for I did not wish to meet a welcoming party of pirates!

So, with the wounded Israel Hands instructing me, I set sail again for Treasure Island.

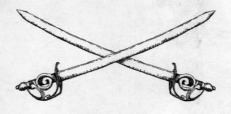

Perhaps two miles out from land I turned the ship to the wind so that we could rest a while. I sat down and began to eat a hasty lunch.

"Jim," says Hands in a pleading tone, but with a crafty look in his eye. "Help your wounded shipmate and go below decks for some wine. Brandy's too strong for a man that's bleeding to death." Plainly, the rogue was at work on some scheme and wanted me out of the way.

"As you say, Mr Hands," says I, for I saw I could play this to my advantage. I stomped down below decks and slipped off my shoes before running silently over to a different hatch and peering out.

I spied that Hands had dragged himself across the deck. He pulled a long knife from a coil of rope, tested the point and hastily hid it in his shirt.

So, I thought, *here we are. Hands may be wounded but he can move. And now he's armed. And he means to kill me. But not before we reach land at least – he can't sail this ship alone.*

I came back on deck with the wine.

"Bless you, Cap'n," said Hands. "I think I'm close to dying. But we'll make it to land."

And then what? thought I, as he began to shout out directions again. I ran around the deck, setting the sails, with one eye on Hands all the while. We covered the two miles fast enough and soon we were cutting through the shoals of a narrow inlet, myself at the tiller. With no anchor we would run the ship aground, and as we drew close to the beach I tensed against the collision.

In those moments I clean forgot to keep a lookout for my murderous shipmate. But something made me shiver and turn. Sure enough, Hands was already advancing across the deck towards me, that long knife gripped tight. Our eyes met and we both shouted – he in fury and I in terror. He lunged at me and I leapt aside, letting go of the tiller, which swung over and struck Hands hard across the chest, stopping him a moment.

I dodged out of the corner he had me in and made for the mast, where I drew out my gun, took aim at Hands, and fired. Nothing! The seawater had dampened the powder. Cursing myself for failing to reload my guns sooner, I watched as the red-faced pirate approached. We stood either side of the mast, feinting and dodging one way and the other. It was a game I had played as a young boy, but never for my life!

A great jolt flung us both to the deck; the ship had hit the beach and was now leaning over at forty-five degrees. I jumped into the rigging and clambered up to sit at the crosstrees, half way up the mast. Hands looked up at me, enraged.

I wasted no time reloading my guns, and Hands saw the trouble he was in. He hauled himself up into the rigging and began to climb towards me, his knife between his teeth.

I aimed both my pistols at him. "One more step, Mr Hands," said I, "and I'll shoot you!" He stopped instantly, his face a picture of confusion. At last, with a swallow or two, he spoke.

"Jim," says he pitifully, "I don't have no luck, not I." As he spoke, his right hand went back over his shoulder. The knife sang through the air. I felt a sharp pang, and there I was pinned by the shoulder to the mast. In that horrible moment of pain both my pistols went off. With a choked cry, Israel Hands let go of the rigging and plunged to his death in the water.

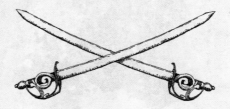

Looking down I saw the body lying on the sea bed, and I shuddered. That very shudder did the business. The knife, in fact, held me by a mere pinch of skin, and it tore free. I climbed back down to the deck and then went below to clean my wound. I sat for a while and rested, waiting for the tide to retreat further and leave me nearer dry land. I thought how overjoyed the others would be at my success and that this would easily overcome their annoyance that I had run off. As the sun set I came back out on deck, climbed down into the now shallow water and splashed ashore.

In good spirits, I set off across the island towards the log house. Soon I came to the place where I had met Ben Gunn and thence on through the trees. It was dark now, and this showed me something strange. Up ahead, about where I judged the log house to be, I could see a warm glow in the sky, as if made by a huge fire.

I tripped and stumbled through the dark towards it and came in time to the clearing and the stockade.

I peered through. There indeed were the embers of a bonfire, which was strange given Captain Smollett's desire to preserve supplies. Not a soul was stirring, though the sound of snoring reached me and I was greatly comforted by this. Thinking I would surprise my companions, I climbed silently over the stockade and approached the house.

It occurred to me that the others were keeping a poor watch and that, had it been the pirates rather than me creeping in, they would all have died.

By this time I had got to the door and stood up. All was dark within. And then, all of a sudden, a shrill voice broke forth out of the darkness.

"Pieces of eight! Pieces of eight! Pieces of eight!" The parrot!

I turned to run and tumbled straight into Long John Silver.

CHAPTER NINE
The Enemy's Camp

There were six remaining pirates, including one who was badly wounded, with a bandage around his head. They had possession of the log house, and of my companions there was no sign.

"So," said Silver, "here's Jim Hawkins, shiver my timbers! Dropped in, eh? Mighty friendly!" Thereupon he sat down across the brandy cask and began to fill a pipe.

"I says you were smart when first I set my eyes on you," he went on. "But this here gets away from me clean, it do."

I stood silent, back to the wall.

"Now, you see, Jim, here's how I sees it," says he. "I've always liked you, I have, for a lad of spirit. I always wanted you to join us and now you've got to. Cap'n Smollett and the doctor have done with you. So unless you start a third group by yourself, you'll have to join with Cap'n Silver."

My friends, then, were still alive!

"So you have a choice, my lad," he went on. "I'm not one for telling a man. You decide what's best for you, and then we'll see what happens."

"Well," says I, growing a bit bolder, "if I'm to choose, I declare I have a right to know what's what, and why you're here, and where my friends are."

"Yesterday morning, Mr Hawkins," said Silver, "down came Doctor Livesey with a flag of truce. Says he, 'Cap'n Silver, you're sold out. Ship's gone.' Well, we looked out, and by thunder, the old ship was gone! So we bargained, the doctor and I, and here we are, in the log house with the supplies. As for them, they've tramped; I don't know where's they are."

He drew again quietly at his pipe.

"Is that all?" I asked.

"Well, it's all that you're to hear, my son," returned Silver.

"Well," said I. "Here you are, in a bad way – ship lost, treasure lost, men lost, your whole business gone to wreck – and if you want to know who did it, it was I! I was in the apple barrel the night we sighted land, and I heard you, John, and Israel Hands, who is now at the bottom of the sea, and I told every word you said before the hour was out.

"And as for the ship, it was I who cut her adrift, and it was I who killed the men you had aboard of her, and it was I who brought her where you'll never see her more, not one of you. So kill me, if you please, or spare me. But one thing I'll say, and no more; if you spare me, bygones are bygones, and when you fellows are in court for piracy, I'll save you all I can.

"It is for you to choose. Kill me and do

yourselves no good, or spare me and keep a witness to save you from the gallows."

Silver looked at me very strangely and I could not tell whether it was in anger or admiration.

Another of the men jumped up and pulled a knife.

"Stop there!" cried Silver. "Who are you, Tom Morgan? Maybe you thought you was cap'n here, perhaps."

Morgan paused, but a hoarse murmur rose from the others.

"Tom's right," said one.

"Not a man lays a finger on this boy," shouted Silver.

There was a long pause after this. I stood straight up against the wall, my heart still going like a sledge-hammer, but with a ray of hope now shining in my bosom. Silver leant back calmly against the wall, but he kept one eye on the men who were now whispering in the corner.

Finally, one of the men spoke up. "This crew's not satisfied," said he, "and we've our rights like any crew. So we'll claim our right to step outside for a council."

Out they all went, and Silver leaned forward to me as soon as we were alone.

"Jim Hawkins," he whispered. "That lot are going to get rid of me as cap'n, and when that happens you and I are both as good as dead. Now, you'll stand by me at trial, you say, if I stand by you now. You're my last card, son."

I began dimly to understand.

"You mean all's lost?" I asked.

"Aye, by gum, I do!" he answered. "My ship's gone, my crew's mostly gone and the rest will soon turn on me, and the treasure's gone. That's the size of it. You'll save me from hanging, won't you, Jim?"

I nodded, bewildered that this terrible old pirate was almost begging me for mercy!

"It's a bargain!" cried Long John. "I'm on the squire's side now! But Jim, these men outside mean trouble. And, talking of trouble, why did that doctor give me the map?"

I was speechless!

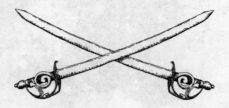

The council outside had lasted some time when the door opened and the five men came in and stood just inside. One stepped forward slowly.

"Step up, lad," cried Silver. "I won't eat you. Hand it over, I know the rules."

The man walked up briskly and handed something to Silver, who looked at what had been given to him.

"The black spot! I thought so," he observed, and turned it over to read the message. "So I'm deposed you say! Perhaps you might be gentlemen and tell me why!"

Here a man with yellowish eyes stepped forward. "Why, you asks? First, you've made a hash of this cruise. Second, you let the enemy out o' this here trap for nothing. Third, you wouldn't let us attack them upon the march. We see your game, Silver; you want to keep all sides happy and see what comes of it. And then, fourth, there's this here boy."

"Is that all, George?" asked Silver quietly. "I made a hash o' this cruise, did I? Well now, you all know I wanted our plans to stay hidden until the treasure was aboard ship. If you'd listened, every man would be alive and we'd be sailing off by now with more gold than you've ever dreamed of."

"That's for point one," cried the accused. "Now about this here boy — isn't he a hostage? He might be our last chance, and I shouldn't wonder. Kill that boy? Not me, mates!"

"And as for striking a bargain with Smollett and his crew, we have a real doctor agreed to visit every day and see them of you that's wounded. But see here, this is what I bargained for."

And with that he pulled a paper from his coat and flung it fluttering on the floor. I recognised it at once and so did the pirates. It was a map with three red crosses on it.

The pirates fell upon it, laughing and cheering. All but one.

"Mighty pretty," said George. "But how are we to get away with no ship?"

Silver suddenly sprang up, supporting himself with a hand against the wall.

"Now I give you warning, George," he cried. "One more word of this and I'll call you down and fight you. How do we get away with no ship? Why, you had ought to tell me that — you and the rest that lost me my schooner, with your impatience, burn you! But you can't tell me, can you? You ain't got the invention of a cockroach. You lost the ship; I found the treasure. Who's the better man at that? Now I resign, by thunder! Elect whom you please to be your cap'n now; I'm done with it."

"Silver!" the others cried. "Silver forever! Silver for cap'n!"

"So that's it?" cried Silver. "George, I reckon you'll have to wait another turn, friend."

That was that, and soon after we laid our heads down to sleep.

I lay for hours lost in thoughts about the remarkable game that I saw Silver now playing — keeping the pirates together with one hand and grasping with the other at me and every other possible means of saving his **neck from the noose.**

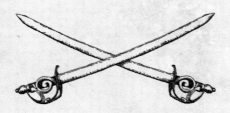

We were all wakened by a clear, hearty voice hailing us from the edge of the wood: "Ahoy!" it cried. "Here's the doctor to see the wounded."

"You, doctor! Top o' the morning to you, sir!" cried Silver, awake and beaming with good nature. "We've quite a surprise for you, sir. We've a little stranger here."

"Not Jim?" said the doctor.

"The very same Jim as ever was," says Silver.

The doctor stopped outright, although he did not speak, and it was some seconds before he seemed able to move on.

"Well, well," he said at last, "duty first and pleasure afterwards, as you might have said yourself, Silver. Let us overhaul these patients of yours."

A moment afterwards he had entered the house and with one grim nod to me proceeded with his work among the sick, checking bandages and such. When that was done he turned again to Silver.

"Well, that's done for today," declared Dr Livesey. "And now I should wish to have a talk with that boy, please."

And he nodded his head in my direction carelessly.

George swung round with a deep flush and cried, "No!"

Silver struck the barrel with his open hand.

"Silence!" he roared and looked about him like a lion. "Doctor," he went on in his usual tones, "we're all humbly grateful for your kindness.

"Hawkins," he said to me, "will you give me your word of honour as a gentleman not to slip your cable?"

I readily gave my word.

"Then, Doctor," said Silver, "you just step outside o' that stockade, and I'll bring the boy down on the inside, and I reckon you can talk through the sticks."

Silver and I walked down to where the doctor awaited us on the other side of the stockade.

"You'll make a note of this here also, Doctor," says he, "and the boy'll tell you how I saved his life and were deposed for it too."

Silver was a changed man. His cheeks looked sunken and his voice trembled.

"Why, John, you're not afraid?" asked Dr Livesey.

"Doctor, I'm no coward, but I've the shakes upon me for the gallows. You're a good man and a true; I never seen a better man! And you'll not forget what I done good, not any more than you'll forget the bad, I know."

So saying, he stepped back a little way to let the doctor and me speak.

"So, Jim," said the doctor sadly, "here you are."

"Doctor," I said, "I should have been dead by now if Silver hadn't stood for me. We've little time. I took the ship. She lies in an inlet at the north of the island."

"The ship!" exclaimed the doctor.

Rapidly I described to him my adventures and he heard me out in silence.

"Every step," said the doctor, "it's you that saves our lives, Jim, and we won't let you lose yours."

"Silver!" he cried. "Three things. First, if you go after that treasure you may expect storms. Second, if we both get out of this I'll do my best to save you from the noose. Third, keep that boy close to you, and if you need help then shout for it. We won't be far away."

With that Dr Livesey shook hands with me through the stockade, nodded to Silver and set off at a brisk pace into the wood.

CHAPTER TEN
Treasure

"Jim," said Silver when we were alone, "if I saved your life, you saved mine; and I'll not forget it. You and me must stick close, back to back like, and we'll save our necks in spite o' fate and fortune."

We rejoined the pirates, and Silver's cunning continued to grow.

"Aye, mates," said he, "it's lucky you have me to think for you. Sure enough, they have the ship. Where they have it, I don't know yet, but once we hit the treasure, we'll have to find out. And then, mates, us that has the shore boats, I reckon, has the upper hand."

"As for our hostage," he continued, "I'll take him on a rope when we go treasure-hunting, for we'll keep him in case of accidents. Once we get the ship and treasure off to sea then we'll talk Mr Hawkins over, we will."

It was no wonder the men were in a good humour now. For my part, I was full of doubts. Silver still had a foot in both camps, and I had no doubt he would prefer wealth and freedom to no gold and a possible hanging.

My heart was uneasy as we all set off to seek the treasure — me joined to Silver by a rope around my waist. We made our way to the beach, climbed into the shore boats and rowed as far inland as we could.

We pulled over and began to climb the tallest of the island's three hills. It was slow, hard work in the heat.

The party spread itself out in a fan shape, shouting and leaping to and fro. We had proceeded thus for about half a mile and were approaching a plateau when one of the men began to cry aloud in terror.

We ran to him and saw him pointing at what lay on the ground. It was a human skeleton, with a few rags of old sailor's clothes. I believe a chill struck for a moment to every heart.

"What sort of way is that for bones to lie?" said Silver. "It don't seem natural." He was right; the bones were laid out so that the form made a line, legs stretched out straight, arms above the head.

"I've taken a notion into my old skull," said Silver, looking at the map. "Here's the compass; there's the top point of the island on the map. It's a pointer! The bones is pointing to the treasure! This here must have been one of the men Flint killed, and he's left him pointing the way."

"Great guns!" he went on. "If Flint was living, this would be a bad spot for us. There were six of them he killed on this island, and there's six of us!"

"I saw him dead," said one of the men.

"Sure enough he's dead and gone below," said another, "but if ever a spirit walked, it would be Flint's. He died bad, did Flint!"

"Aye, that he did," observed another. "I can remember him hollering his only song, *Fifteen Men*, and calling for rum, and singing right up to when he died."

"Stow this talk," said Silver. "Flint's dead, and he don't walk. Now lads, let's get on for the gold!"

We pressed on, but the terror of Flint had fallen on all the pirates' spirits.

We sat down to rest as soon as we reached the plateau. We could see the whole island from here and for miles. Not a sound but the thunder of the surf. Not a sail upon the sea. The solitude added to our unease.

Silver was looking at the map and taking bearings from the compass. The men continued to talk in hushed tones about Flint's terrible life and horrible death.

All of a sudden, out of the middle of the trees in front of us, a thin, high, trembling voice struck up the well-known tune:

"Fifteen men on the dead man's chest –
Yo-ho-ho, and a bottle of rum!"

I never have seen men more dreadfully affected than the pirates. The colour drained from their faces. Some jumped to their feet, some grabbed each other.

"It's Flint, by hell!" cried one.

The song had stopped as suddenly as it began, as though someone had laid his hand upon the singer's mouth.

"Come," said Silver, struggling with his ashen lips to get the word out, "this won't do. I can't name the voice, but it's someone that's flesh and blood."

Calm was returning, but then the same voice broke out again – not singing, but in a faint distant cry that echoed around the hills.

"Darby M'Graw," it wailed, "Darby M'Graw! Darby M'Graw!"

Long after the voice had died away the pirates still stared in silence, full of dread.

"That fixes it!" gasped one. "Let's go."

Still Silver was unconquered.

"Shipmates," he cried with a great effort, "I'm here to get that stuff, and I'll not be beat by man or devil. I never was feared of Flint in his life, and, by the powers, I'll face him dead. There's seven hundred thousand pound not a quarter of a mile from here."

But the others were too terrified even to speak.

"Now that voice had an echo," he said. "What's a spirit doing with an echo?"

This argument seemed weak to me. But you can never tell what will affect the superstitious, and, to my wonder, the pirates were greatly relieved.

"Well, that's true," said George. "And it sounded like Flint but not perfect. It sounded like someone else but I can't think who …"

"By the powers — Ben Gunn!" roared Silver.

"Aye, and so it were," cried another, springing to his feet. "Ben Gunn it were! And nobody fears Ben Gunn, dead or alive!"

It was extraordinary how instantly their spirits had returned, and we were soon off again, following Silver's directions as he read the map, which instructed us to look for a tall tree.

There was no mistaking the tree when we drew close. A huge red trunk rose nearly two hundred feet in the air. The thought of the money, as they grew nearer, swallowed up the pirates' previous terrors.

Silver hobbled on his crutch. His eyes blazed and he tugged furiously at the line that held me to him. I read his thoughts like print. With so much gold near at hand, Silver would forget all promises, get the treasure aboard ship and cut my throat.

We reached the shadow of the tree and looked about. George shouted and the men ran forward. Then they stopped, silent. Silver

doubled his pace and next moment he and I had come also to a dead halt.

Before us was a great hole, not very recent, for the sides had fallen in and grass had sprouted from the earth. At the bottom was a piece of board branded with one word: WALRUS. The seven hundred thousand pounds were gone!

CHAPTER ELEVEN
The Return

Everything changed in an instant. The pirates were stunned for a moment. But with Silver the blow passed almost instantly. Every thought of his soul had been set on that gold and he was brought up short. Yet he kept his head and changed his plan before the others had even begun to realise the disappointment.

"Jim," he whispered, "take that, and stand by for trouble."

"So you've changed sides once more," I whispered, revolted at his constant changes.

He passed me a double-barrelled pistol.

The pirates leaped into the pit and scrabbled in the dirt with their fingers. George found a two guinea piece.

"Two guineas!" he roared at Silver. "That's your seven hundred thousand pounds, is it?"

"Dig away, boys," said Silver. "You'll find some pig-nuts, I shouldn't wonder."

The pirates scrambled out of the pit again and stood opposite us. Silver never moved; he watched them, very upright on his crutch, and looked as cool as ever I saw him. He was brave, and no mistake.

"At 'em, boys!" George thundered. "Cut 'em down!"

But just then – crack! crack! crack! – three musket-shots flashed out of the trees. Two of the men tumbled dead into the pit and the other three turned and ran for it with all their might.

At the same moment, the doctor, Gray and Ben Gunn emerged from the trees with smoking muskets.

"Forward!" cried the doctor. "Double quick, my lads. We must head 'em off before they get to the boats."

We set off at a great pace, Silver anxious to keep up with us. The work that man went through, leaping on his crutch till the muscles of his chest were fit to burst, was work no man ever equalled; and so thinks the doctor.

"Doctor," called Silver in a while, "see there! No hurry!"

Sure enough, we could see the three survivors still running in the same direction as they had started.

We were already between them and the boats, and so we four sat down to breathe, while Long John, mopping his face, came slowly up with us.

"Thank ye kindly, doctor," says he. "You came just in time for me and Hawkins. And so it's you, Ben Gunn!" he added. "Ben, Ben, to think it's you who's done me!"

We proceeded downhill at a more leisurely pace and the doctor related his story.

Ben Gunn in his long, lonely wanderings

about the island had found the treasure, had dug it up and had carried it on his back, in many weary journeys, to a cave he used. There it had lain stored in safety since two months before the arrival of the *Hispaniola*.

When the doctor had learned of this from Ben he had gone to Silver, made his bargain, handed over the now useless map and left the house and stores. The party stayed instead in Ben's cave, where the treasure lay, along with plenty more rations.

When he learned that I was to be present when the pirates discovered the treasure had been taken, the doctor raced back to the cave and brought Ben Gunn and Gray to lie in wait.

"Ah," said Silver, "it were fortunate for me that I had Hawkins here. Else, you would have let old John be cut to bits by his shipmates and never given it a thought, Doctor."

"Not a thought," replied Dr Livesey cheerfully.

By this time we had reached the shore boats. The doctor, with the pick-axe, demolished one of them, and then we all got aboard the other and set out to go round by sea to the north of the island.

This was a run of eight or nine miles. As we came into the inlet we found the *Hispaniola*, cruising by herself. The tide had lifted her, and had there been much wind or a strong current she might have drifted out to sea! As it was, there was little amiss with the ship. Another anchor was got ready and dropped, and then we pulled the shore boat around to a beach beneath Ben's cave.

A gentle slope ran up from the beach to the entrance of the cave. At the top, the squire met us. To me he was cordial and kind, saying nothing of my escapade either in the way of blame or praise. But at Silver's polite salute he grew angry.

"John Silver," he said, "you're a monstrous villain, sir. I am told I am not to prosecute you. But the dead men, sir, hang about your neck like mill-stones."

"Thank you kindly, sir," replied Long John, again saluting.

Thereupon we all entered the cave. It was a large, airy place. Before a big fire lay Captain Smollett, and in a far corner, flickered over by the blaze, I beheld great heaps of coin and bars of gold. That was Flint's treasure that we had come so far to seek and that had cost already the lives of seventeen men from the *Hispaniola*.

What a supper I had of it that night, with all my friends around me, and what a meal it was, with Ben Gunn's salted goat. There was Silver, sitting back almost out of the firelight, but eating heartily, prompt to spring forward when anything was wanted, even joining quietly in our laughter — the same polite, charming old seaman who set sail with us from Bristol.

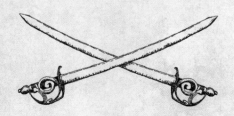

The next day we set to work counting and loading the gold on board ship. Day after day this work went on and, by every evening, another fortune had been stowed.

We elected to leave the three remaining pirates on the island, to Ben Gunn's obvious glee. We left provisions and tools and weapons for them in the cave.

Finally, early one bright morning, we boarded the *Hispaniola* and set sail. Before noon, to my utmost joy, the highest rock of Treasure Island had sunk into the blue round of the sea.

We sailed for the nearest port in Spanish America, for we could not risk the voyage home without a larger and fresher crew, and by the time we reached land again we were all worn out from manning the ship with so few of us.

It was just at sundown when we cast anchor in a most beautiful land-locked gulf and were immediately surrounded by shore boats full of locals selling fruits and vegetables. The sight of so many happy faces, the taste of the tropical fruits and, above all, the lights that began to shine in the town made a most charming contrast to our dark and bloody memories of the island.

The following morning, a bag of three or four hundred guineas and Long John Silver had both gone missing. I think we were all pleased to be so cheaply rid of him.

Well, we got a few new men on board and the *Hispaniola* made a good cruise back to Bristol. Five men only of those who had sailed returned with her.

All of us had an ample share of the treasure and used it wisely or foolishly, according to our natures. Captain Smollett is now retired from the sea. Gray saved his money and he is now part owner of a fine ship. As for Ben Gunn, he got a thousand pounds, which he spent or lost in three weeks, or to be more exact, in nineteen days, for he was back begging on the twentieth.

Of Silver we have heard no more. That formidable seafaring man with one leg has at last gone clean out of my life – but I dare say he met his wife and perhaps still lives in comfort with her and his parrot.

Who can say what further treasure still lies buried on the island – the map showed three places and we raided only one. But what remains will remain forever for all I care. Nothing could drag me back to that cursed island. In my worst dreams I still hear the surf booming, the pirates singing and Silver's parrot screaming out, "Pieces of eight! Pieces of eight! Pieces of eight!"